N

A Play

by

Adrienne Earle Pender

Published by
Blue Moon Plays

ISBN: 978-1-943416-40-0
Manufactured in United States of America
Cover Designer: Maggie Douglas
Editor: Jean Klein

Published by Blue Moon Plays, LLC
4876-118 Princess Anne Rd
Virginia Beach, VA 23462
Printed in the USA

N

This script can be performed by community, educational, or professional theaters either for the stage, the classroom, or as reader's theater.

Copyright law prevents this script from being copied or shared by any technical or digital means.

If you wish to perform this play, you must do the following:
- Purchase sufficient copies of this play for your cast and crew at Blue Moon Plays (www.havescripts.com). Scripts are available as a printable PDF download (MutiCopy PDF) or as hard copies at an automatic discount for multiple orders.
- Apply for a performance license.
- Purchase a performance license for the specific days of your performance .

Performance Rights must be purchased, approved, and licensed by Blue Moon Plays.

If you wish to make changes in the script of any kind, you must receive permission from the publisher or the playwright.

All materials associated with the production—programs, advertising, licensing, etc.—must include the name of the playwright in font no less the ½ the size of the font.

**For information,
visit www.havescripts.com
email inbasket@bluemoonplays.com or
call 757-816-1164**

N

CAST OF CHARACTERS

Charles S. Gilpin - African-American male, 35-40 (40 at the start of the play).

Charles is an average size and build, but he has confidence, and a presence. He's intelligent, somewhat sophisticated, and always looks sharp. Charles lives and dies by his emotions but also knows how to live in his very segregated times.

Eugene O'Neill - Caucasian male, 35-40 (37 at the start of the play)

O'Neill, the brooding master playwright, early in his career. He is brilliant, cynical, and dryly sarcastic; he doesn't smile or laugh easily so when he does it is noticeable. He is also a sharp dresser, as was typical for men in that time.

Florence Gilpin - African-American female, 25-30 (30 at the start of the play)

Florence is Charles's wife. She's pretty and curvy. She is the woman behind the man who is proud of the man she loves but tries to keep him grounded.

SETTINGS

- Representative kitchen area in the home of Charles and Florence Gilpin (small table, 2 chairs, down Stage Right)
- The theater, in various stages of *The Emperor Jones* production (main area, Center Stage)
- Office desk area at the theater (small, down Stage Left, alternates with Podium area for Drama League)

All three representative areas are set and visible; actors move and lights change when in use, dark when not in use.

SCENES

ACT ONE

Scene 1	Fall 1920
Scene 2	One month later; the day before The Emperor Jones opening
Scene 3	One week later; a week after the opening
Scene 4	February, 1921; the Drama League controversy

ACT TWO

Scene 1	Fall, 1923; two years later
Scene 2	March, 1924; six months later
Scene 3	November 1926; 2 years later
Scene 4	Epilogue

ACT 1
Scene 1

September, 1920, flashback – 6 months prior.

The lights come up down Stage Right, on the kitchen area in the home of CHARLES and FLORENCE GILPIN, stage Right. There is a small table and 2 chairs, a throw rug, and perhaps a small cupboard .

FLORENCE, 30ish, curvy and pretty, is wearing her coat and hat, has just come home from her domestic work. She faces Stage Right, addressing someone off-stage.

FLORENCE: (Calling) Thank you, again, for staying late with the baby, Mrs. Cooper!

> (Florence drops into one of the chairs in the kitchen, exhausted. She closes her eyes, takes a deep breath, and exhales. She takes another deep breath, and exhales. That's all the 'rest' she allows herself.
>
> She gets up, takes off her coat and hat, puts on an apron, and immediately gets to her own home's work, folding clothes in a laundry basket.
>
> CHARLES bursts into the room, excitedly. He's just come from an audition.)

CHARLES: FLORENCE! You won't believe what just happened!

FLORENCE: WHAT??

CHARLES: I got a part in a play – a big part!

FLORENCE: WHAT??!? How??

CHARLES: The Emperor Jones, by Eugene O'Neill!

FLORENCE: Ain't heard'a him before.

1

CHARLES: He's a playwright in one of those new theaters downtown! He's a white man.

FLORENCE: A white man is gonna let you – in his play?

CHARLES: YES, baby!

FLORENCE: But -- YOU'RE A NEGRO!

CHARLES: Yeah -- I KNOW!

FLORENCE: It must be a little part ...

> (Charles hands her the script)

FLORENCE: (Reading) "The Emperor Jones. By Eugene O'Neill, produced by the Provincetown Players."

CHARLES: Florence – it's the lead. I'M playing the Emperor Jones!!

FLORENCE: (Sits down, stunned) NO.

CHARLES: YES!!

> (He grabs her, and starts to dance)

CHARLES: Who needs Bessie Smith? We can make our own music right now!

FLORENCE: HUSH, Charles! You'll wake the baby!

CHARLES: Wake him up! And you tell him his daddy has made it!

FLORENCE: If you wake him up, YOU put him back to sleep.

> (Charles stops humming, pauses – and then keeps dancing)

FLORENCE: I thought so.

CHARLES: He's gonna be proud of his daddy one day.

(Florence stops dancing and steps back)

FLORENCE: He'll be proud of you no matter what.

(Charles kisses her hands)

FLORENCE: So how much does it pay?

CHARLES: (Pulling her leg) Huh?

FLORENCE: How much – does this – starring role PAY?

CHARLES: (Enjoying this) Pay?

FLORENCE: Oh I KNOW you're not doing this for free!

CHARLES: Shush now, 'you'll wake the baby!'

(Florence laughs, and tries to hit him; he dodges her
and she chases him)

CHARLES: Fifty dollars!

(She stops in her tracks)

FLORENCE: Say that again?

CHARLES: It pays fifty dollars. (Pauses for effect) A WEEK.

(Florence sits down, stunned)

FLORENCE: I don't believe it.

CHARLES: I promised you I'd take care of you; and now I can.

FLORENCE: I always knew you would. I just didn't think it would be
from…. Acting!

3

CHARLES: (Laughs, but then seriously) Neither did I. I'm forty years old, and I can finally be proud of something!

FLORENCE: Fifty dollars a week, that's real money!

CHARLES: The show might not run but a few weeks; it's only scheduled for a month. That's only $200.00

FLORENCE: ONLY?

CHARLES: You can't quit your job yet – but we can catch up.

FLORENCE: I worked all my life, and I WILL work all my life, ain't no changing that. But, maybe we can save a little... for the baby?

CHARLES: And... Maybe, we can have another baby?

FLORENCE: (Lowers her head, giggles) CHARLES!!

CHARLES: I don't want you working for white folks, cleaning their houses. I want you here, in our home.

FLORENCE: Well we aren't there yet.

CHARLES: YET.

FLORENCE: So how did all this happen??

> (Florence sits in the chair, and lights dim around her while Charles, in spotlight, tells the story. As he regales her with the details, sounds of elevator doors opening and closing are heard)

CHARLES: I'm doing my job at Macy's, just working the elevator like I always do. White folks get on and off the elevator all the time, so I don't pay attention anymore, and after lunch, this man gets on the elevator – and he says,

VOICEOVER: Are you Charles Gilpin?

CHARLES: YES.... (Announcing) Second floor, ladies underthings, corsets. He said,

VOICEOVER: I'm from the Provincetown Players, and we have a good part for you in a new play by O'Neill.

CHARLES: I said, 'EUGENE O'Neill?' (Announcing) Third floor, draperies, upholsteries, linens.

VOICEOVER: That's him!

CHARLES: He says... 'How good is the part?' I say. (Announcing) Fourth Floor, furniture.'

VOICEOVER: The lead –

CHARLES: He says.... I say, 'what's the pay?' (Announcing) Fifth floor, Bedding, bathroom supplies.

VOICEOVER: We can only pay $50 a week... but wouldn't you like to act again?

CHARLES: And I said, 'YES! Yes I would! Who are you, and where do I go??' Then he said,

VOICEOVER: I'm Jasper Deeter.

> (Spotlight fades and lights come back up to normal over Florence)

CHARLES: ...and he took me down to Macdougal Street, where the Provincetown Players theater is. They gave me a script and gave me a few minutes to look over the scene. It was great, I could see that right away.... O'Neill is quiet, he doesn't say much. But his words on paper... I've never seen words like that before. Brutus was an ex-Pullman Porter, like me! He worked hard, had odd jobs all his life, like me. I knew him. Baby, I knew him right away! Jasper said, 'do you want me to read with you?' and I said no.... I'd read the start of the monologue, if that was fine with them. And I barely looked at the script. I started, and my shoulders went back, and my voice rose, and all the noise in the theater stopped. EVERYTHING stopped. And I was IN the jungle, scared for my life and before I knew it, the monologue was over... and O'Neill asked me why I stopped. He just – stared at me. And then he said, 'the part is yours. Can you start rehearsals tomorrow?'

FLORENCE: Oh Charles…..

CHARLES: The lead. (Pause) There's a white man in the Provincetown Players, named Charles Ellis – HE wanted the part too, wanted to play it in blackface, like all the other theaters do these days. Jasper saw me in the *Abraham Lincoln* play, then he brought O'Neill and another man to see it. Thank God I felt Brutus today! I took that part right outta that white man's hands!!

FLORENCE: I can't believe it…

CHARLES: This part…. It feels… I don't know, I can't explain it… I know his struggle. There are Brutus Joneses all over Harlem every day, I see them; men just wanting to be – more – than they are, just waiting for their chance to be something great. (Pause) The script is – well you know white folks, they think they know how we talk – O'Neill puts a lot of 'dems' and 'deres' for 'them' and 'there,' it's all over the place.

FLORENCE: Like we're ALL ignorant, and still slaves. I was polishing silver today, and Mrs. Mason comes in and decides to tell me how to do it "properly," and she spoke real loud and slow, like I didn't understand English. Woman, I was born here, just like you were! And I been polishing silver all my life, I know what to do!

CHARLES: I know you didn't say that to her!

FLORENCE: Of course not, I said, 'yes, ma'am,' like I always do.

CHARLES: He has a lot of that word in the script too.

FLORENCE: (Cautiously) Charles….

CHARLES: <u>They</u> call us... nigger... so they think we call each other that, too. We don't talk like that. But I can fix it.

FLORENCE: You're not going to fix anything. This is a chance a colored man might never have again.

CHARLES: I can finally show the world what I can do!

FLORENCE: And you will! But do the job they hired you to do!

CHARLES: This O'Neill... he's different. If I do this right, other white writers might give chances to more Negro actors. It feels like – like everything is going to be different after this.

FLORENCE: Are you listening to me?? Do what they tell you to do; and go where they tell you to go. It's his script; say the lines he wrote. And stay away from the bottle, you hear me?

CHARLES: I'll be fine.

FLORENCE: DO. YOU. <u>HEAR</u>. ME? (Silence) Just say yes, ma'am.

(Charles just looks at her)

BLACKOUT

END OF SCENE

ACT 1 Scene 2

October, 1920; rehearsal, the day before opening night. The center and main portion of the stage is devoted to a portion of The Emperor Jones set. The scene being rehearsed is Scene 3, a jungle scene, so there should be facsimiles of some trees and brush. Since this is a rehearsal there can been typical last-minute stage items, like a ladder or lights to be hung.

Charles is alone, center stage, only partially dressed in his Brutus Jones costume.

CHARLES: Jeff! Jeff, is that you?

EUGENE: (VOICE ONLY)STOP!!

CHARLES: Why?

> (EUGENE O'NEILL stands from sitting in the aisle a few rows back in the audience (or from mid-house), and descends slowly. He is careful and measured, and is dressed in a suit)

EUGENE: What are you doing?

CHARLES: I thought I was acting.　　　　　　(Remembers his place) Sir.

EUGENE: You were OVER-acting. Sir.

CHARLES: I was – attempting a different emotion there, certainly, but –

EUGENE: Do you think I don't know over-acting when I see it?

CHARLES: I don't know... do you?

EUGENE: You're not intimidated, that's good.

CHARLES: No need to be, sir.

EUGENE: No more 'sir,' alright?

CHARLES: Alright.

EUGENE: And I do know a little about over-acting. My father was the KING of over-actors.

> (Charles laughs, and in spite of himself, Eugene smiles)

CHARLES: Your father – James O'Neill.

EUGENE: You've done your homework.

CHARLES: Of course.

EUGENE: Did you ever see him on stage?

CHARLES: (Matter-of-factly) No.

EUGENE: Oh??

CHARLES: I doubt he played in theaters I could attend...

EUGENE: (It takes him a beat or two to 'get it') Oh. Oh, yes, certainly... Well, he definitely played everywhere else in the country.

CHARLES: Was he good? Besides the over-acting, I mean.

EUGENE: He could have been. He probably was, once. But he played this one part – The Count of Monte Christo – for years. Do you know the play?

CHARLES: No, I don't.

EUGENE: It's about a man whose life was stolen from him. He was wrongly imprisoned, escapes after a long time in jail, makes a fortune, and returns to his home a rich man, to seek vengeance on those who stole his life from him.

CHARLES: Vengeance has consequences.

EUGENE: It does, indeed. And there's also hope, and justice, and forgiveness, and all that nonsense in the play.

CHARLES: Forgiveness isn't nonsense.

EUGENE: I haven't got time for forgiveness

CHARLES: Colored people live our lives practicing forgiveness, every minute of every day. (Pause) So this part of the Count, it had everything?

EUGENE: Yes I suppose... Lots of meat for an actor to play with.

CHARLES: Maybe that's why he liked the part?

EUGENE: Oh, no doubt. He liked it too much; but he got comfortable and, I think, lazy. After a while it's all he played, that one part. And, after a while, it was only part that anyone wanted to see him in, ever. He played it, easily over 5,000 times. Eventually he couldn't do anything else. It ended up destroying him.

CHARLES: You think so?

EUGENE: Oh I KNOW so. (Pause) And now it's up to history to judge whether "the great" James O'Neill was ever really great.

CHARLES: History....

EUGENE: My father died a few months ago.

CHARLES: Oh I am very sorry – I had no idea.

EUGENE: You wouldn't.

CHARLES: He knew you made it, though. I'm sure he was proud of you.

(Pause)

EUGENE: We aren't here to talk about me.

CHARLES: No.

EUGENE: Start from where we left off. And Charlie – say ALL the words as written this time, PLEASE.

(Eugene steps back several feet out of the way, down Stage Left, and watches Charles)

(Charles turns his back to the house, inhales, exhales, and takes his moment to prepare. His shoulders drop. He IS Brutus Jones. It is a full, complete, complex performance.

In this excerpt from The Emperor Jones, except where *italicized*, the directions within the monologue come directly from the play)

CHARLES/BRUTUS:

"What time's it getting' to be, I wonder? I dassent light no match to find out. Phoo! It's warm an' dat's a fac! [Wearily} How long I been makin' tracks in dese woods? Must be hours an' hours. Seems like fo'evah! Yit can't be, when dey moon's jes' riz. [A mournful chuckle] Majesty! Der ain't much majesty 'bout dis baby now. Never min... It's all part o'le game. Dis night come to an end like everything else. And when you gits dar safe and has dat bankroll in yo' hands you laughs at all dis. [He starts to whistle but checks himself abruptly]. What yo whistlin' for, you po' dope? Want all de worl' to heah you? [He stops talking to listen] Heah dat ole drum? Sho gits nearer from de sound.

A drumbeat – the tom-tom – begins, for Charles and the audience. The drumbeat is low and steady. Charles noticeably reacts to hearing the tom-tom.

Dey're packin it along wid 'em. Time fo' me to move. [He takes a step forward, then stops, worriedly] What's dat odd clickety sound I heah? Dere it is! Sound close! Sound like – sound like – Fo'God sake, sound like some – Ni -- {CHARLES PAUSES} Nigger – was shootin' crap! I better beat it quick when I gits dem notions! [Brutus walks quickly into the clear space – then stands transfixed as he thinks he sees someone in the distance] Who dat? Who dat? Is dat you,

11

Jeff? [Starting toward 'Jeff', forgets his surroundings, in happy relief] Jeff! I'se sho' mighty glad to see you! Dey tol' me you done died from dat razor cut I gives you. [Stops, bewildered] But how you come to be heah? [He stares at 'Jeff', then starts to roll his eyes wildly, his body sways] Ain't you gwine – look up – can't you speak to me? Is you – is you – a ha'nt? [He jerks out his revolver in a frenzy of terror and rage] Nigger {*CHARLES SAYS IT DELIBERATELY*} I kills you dead once. Has I got to kill you again? You take it, den! [He fires the gun. 'Jeff vanishes. Brutus stands, trembling but reassured] He's gone, anyway. Ha'nt or no Ha'nt, dat shot fix him. [The beat of the tom-tom is perceptively louder and more rapid. Brutus becomes conscious of it – with a start he looks over his shoulder] Dey's gittin' near! Dey's comin' fast! And heah I is shootin' shots to let 'em know jes whar I is. Oh, Gorry, I'se got to run! [Forgetting the path he turns and starts to run wildly into the jungle.]

> (As Brutus/Charles turns to run, Eugene takes a step, clearly impressed)

EUGENE: That's really good.

> (Charles turns back around, panting, halfway back from being Brutus Jones. The tom-tom fades out. His eyes fix on Eugene, and after a minute he calms himself)

CHARLES: Yes, I think that will work.

EUGENE: That was…. Wonderful, actually.

CHARLES: Thank you, sir. (Eugene 'looks' at him) I'm sorry, the sir seemed appropriate.

EUGENE: And when we add the drums in, it will be spot on.

CHARLES: (Still coming back to being Charles) I heard drums, yes…

EUGENE: Charlie?

CHARLES: Didn't you HEAR – there were drums...

> (Eugene looks at Charles for a moment, as Charles comes fully back)

EUGENE: You stumbled once.

CHARLES: Yes. Yes, I did. It's that word.

EUGENE: Not again.

CHARLES: We don't say that word.

EUGENE: We?

CHARLES: Colored people. We don't like that word. I'm sorry – but that's a word white people call us.

EUGENE: I'm fairly certain I've heard a Negro call another Negro 'nigger' before.

CHARLES: We have – we do... But it's not the same thing.

EUGENE: Why isn't it the same?

CHARLES: Because for us, it's – it's a connection to an experience that we all share. We say that word to another Negro, and it an understanding that we are connected.

EUGENE: Where as, for White people, it's –

CHARLES: (Cutting him off) Racist.

EUGENE: Always?

CHARLES: When White people say it, it's said in derision. You use it to demean us, to remove as a class, and strip our humanity. It's only ever a word of hate for you.

13

(Eugene looks at Charles but says nothing)

EUGENE: But not every Negro uses it.

CHARLES: No. There's so much hate around that word, that many of us won't say it at all.

(Pause)

EUGENE: Well then, I think Brutus WOULD say it, and now I think he might say it even more than I have it in the play.

CHARLES: I think you're wrong.

EUGENE: Oh you do?

CHARLES:
With respect … yes, I think Brutus is smarter than that.

EUGENE: He'd want to relate to the Negroes on the island. And ultimately, he lets superstition and fear get the better of him.

CHARLES: But he was smart enough to take over this island and make these people think he was an emperor. He wouldn't need that vernacular to do it.

EUGENE: You've _really_ thought about this.

CHARLES: I have, yes.

EUGENE: And you think you know him better than I do?

(Charles knows he's stepped over the line)

CHARLES: (Clear sucking up) Oh no, I wouldn't say _better_, not at all. It's such a good part, and the writing is so good that – I just know him very well. Mr. O'Neill.

EUGENE: Well that's a good answer.

14

(Charles laughs too)

EUGENE: Mr. O'Neill was my father, I keep telling you to call me Gene.

CHARLES: I don't know if I can do that.

EUGENE: Well you'd better damn well try.

(Pause)

EUGENE: You know... I think you are going to surprise a lot of people.

CHARLES: Why? Do people think Negroes can't act?

EUGENE: I didn't say that.

CHARLES: You didn't SAY it...

EUGENE: If I really though that way, you wouldn't be here.

CHARLES: If I didn't say it before – thank you.

EUGENE: Don't thank me. You earned it.

CHARLES: You wrote a part... the part of a lifetime. A part worthy of ANY actor, but for a Negro... well I've waited my whole life for a part this good. So yes, I do have to thank you – Gene.

EUGENE: Thank YOU, Charlie. (Pause) I mean that.

> (They look at each other for a long moment, then look around and walk the stage, look out into the 'house,' take it all in... and then back at each other again)

CHARLES: Are you ready for all this?

EUGENE: No... A theater on opening night is no place for a nervous man.

CHARLES: You've done this before, why should you be nervous?

EUGENE: The play in a playwright's head is rarely what appears on the stage. It's just better not to subject myself to that.

CHARLES: Have you ever thought about directing? You'd be good, actually.

EUGENE: Condescension notwithstanding.

CHARLES: (Lying) I didn't mean to be condescending; I've worked with a lot of directors. You don't say much in rehearsal, but you're observant. Nothing gets by you.

EUGENE: No. I thought about it once, but no. I write plays... "Theater" is something different.

CHARLES: What is it?

EUGENE: Theater... is someone else's translation of what they think a play is; it's not necessarily the writer's intention. Theater is for the masses; it's just the way the story gets out.

CHARLES: Well, tomorrow night this theater will be full of 'the masses.'

EUGENE: Are YOU ready for all this?

CHARLES: Gene – I've BEEN ready.

> (They step towards each other, center stage, with respect and excitement. Charles offers his hand; Eugene looks at it, and then takes it, and they shake hands)

> BLACKOUT

> END OF SCENE

ACT ONE Scene 3

CHARLES and FLORENCE'S kitchen, November 8, 1921; one week after the opening of The Emperor Jones. Florence is in her work dress and apron, sitting at the kitchen table. The reviews are in!

Newspapers are scattered on the table, and Florence is reading slowly from one review.

FLORENCE: (Reading to Charles, who is offstage)
"...Also, if The Emperor Jones were taken elsewhere we have little doubt that the manager would engage a white man with a piece of burnt cork to play Brutus Jones. They have done better in Macdougal Street. The Emperor is played by a Negro actor named Charles S. Gilpin, who gives the most thrilling performance we have seen any place this season. He sustains the succession of scenes in monologue not only because his voice is one of gorgeous natural quality – "
(Charles interrupts from off-stage)

CHARLES: (Calling, laughing and proud) Gorgeous what?

FLORENCE: 'Gorgeous natural quality!'

(Charles laughs boisterously)

FLORENCE: (Continues reading)
"... but because he knows just what to do with it... One performance is not enough to entitle a player to the word great even from a not too careful critic, but there can be no question whatever that in The Emperor Jones Gilpin is great. It is a performance of heroic stature..."

(Charles enters, in dress pants and untucked shirt, wiping his hands on a towel. He carries a bottle of whiskey and a glass)

FLORENCE: There's another paragraph about how the play should end, but we don't have to read that again.

CHARLES: (He knows the answer) What paper was that in?

FLORENCE: That was the New York Tribune.

CHARLES: Read that last part about me again...

FLORENCE: "...but there can be no question whatever that in The Emperor Jones Gilpin is great. It is a performance of heroic stature."

CHARLES: "Heroic stature."

CHARLES: (Picks up another paper)
"Though this new play of O'Neill's is so clumsily ... it weaves a most potent spell, thank partly to the force and cunning of its author, thanks partly to the admirable playing of Charles S. Gilpin... His is an uncommonly powerful and imaginative performance, in several respects unsurpassed this season in New York..."
That's from the New York Times!!

FLORENCE: You've done it!!

CHARLES: Now everybody knows it!

FLORENCE: I went out for milk earlier today, and Mr. Andrews offered me store credit for the groceries! He said it was an honor to have you has a customer. I'll never use it, but —

CHARLES: Yes you WILL use it!

FLORENCE: It's dangerous to spend money we might not have next month.

CHARLES: We have it now.

FLORENCE: He's so proud of you, everyone is talking about you! And your Son is gonna know his daddy was somebody, he'll be proud of you too!

CHARLES: And what about you... Are you proud of me?

FLORENCE: I don't need a newspaper to be proud of you.

CHARLES: The papers – we have to save these.

FLORENCE: Absolutely!!

CHARLES: Gene says that the Provincetown Players are overbooked; they went from 200 members to 1500 members just since last week. And now that the reviews are out? We're the hottest ticket in town! All of New York is clamoring to see me.

FLORENCE: To see the play...

CHARLES: To see ME play Brutus Jones. You read them; the reviews had some problems with the play, none of them have a problem with me. (He picks up and shakes several papers) Not a single one!

FLORENCE: Do you really want ALL the reviews?

CHARLES: All the good ones

FLORENCE: Because this one from the Negro paper says that The Emperor Jones "plays to the worst of Negro stereotypes..."

CHARLES: I know what they say.

FLORENCE: And, "Negro World" says that, "... it is pronounced a great play by the critics; but they are white, and they will pronounce anything good that has white supremacy as its theme."

CHARLES: (Standing) I KNOW what they say. How can I take a role like this, a thief and a murderer; it does nothing to lift up our race. They don't understand... (He's going through the argument in his head) No one play – no one role – can do EVERYTHING! It can't answer every question, or address every issue, or right every wrong. There's never been a role like this, for US, and showing what a Negro actor can DO will only help all of us, no matter what that role is.

FLORENCE: No matter what it may cost you?

CHARLES: Cost?

FLORENCE: I just know how many years it took you to break out of playing in minstrel shows. Is Brutus Jones any better than that?

CHARLES: Of course it's better!

FLORENCE: Why? Because a white man wrote it?

CHARLES: Brutus is a Negro, but he represents all men. (Pauses, thinking) Brutus is a bully, but all races have Bullies. The bigger the bully, the bigger the coward. Brutus is superstitious; but all races have superstitions in their core. Superstition is merely ignorance, and all people are more or less ignorant about something; that doesn't apply to just one race.

FLORENCE: You're right.

CHARLES: I know I am. The character may not be worthy – but the role IS worthy. No matter the cost.

FLORENCE: Okay, you win! And your performance is MORE than worthy. Everyone thinks you're brilliant.

CHARLES: I've gotta do something with this. I have to find a way to make this last.

FLORENCE: You have to finish this play, first. Then, whatever happens, will happen.

CHARLES: (He pours another drink) Everyone will want to work with me now...

FLORENCE: Oh, you think that other parts will just fall out of the sky for a Negro actor?

CHARLES: This play is... epic. Who knows what could be coming for us?

FLORENCE: The world isn't going to change because of one play.

CHARLES: It might!

FLORENCE: Honey, white theaters will keep doing what they do NOW; hire white actors for Negro roles, and blacken 'em up. Blackface isn't ending with you.

CHARLES: Are you trying to ruin this day for me?

FLORENCE: I'm trying to remind you that this play has only three more weeks before it's over, and then you and I go back to "real" life – Negro communities in this country still smoldering from the Red Summer.

CHARLES: Two dozen communities on fire because of race in this country, I don't need to be reminded about that. Fifty-three Negroes lynched last year in this country, I do not need to be reminded about that!

FLORENCE: And YOU have never been allowed to vote in this country, even though it's supposed to be legal for you to do it. So, my darling, one day next month, the Provincetown Players will start rehearsing their next play, and they will move on. I'm sure Mr. O'Neill is already working on his next play. All this attention will be gone, and I'll be cleaning houses just like I am now, and you'll be back at Macy's working the elevator.

CHARLES: They might extend the run – there's talk already that it might even move to Broadway.

FLORENCE: Don't get ahead of yourself.

CHARLES: I thought you were proud of me.

FLORENCE: I love you, of course I'm proud of you.

CHARLES: You've got a strange way of showing it.

FLORENCE: Listen to me. You have done something none of us has ever done before. We are more than just dancing, singing fools, and that's because of you. No one will EVER take that from you.

CHARLES: You love me.

FLORENCE: Yeah... I do. (He drinks) Charlie.

CHARLES: I'm celebrating!

FLORENCE: There are all kinds of ways to celebrate...

CHARLES: This is my way.

FLORENCE: You have this opportunity, this—once in a LIFETIME opportunity –

CHARLES: It's not once in a lifetime.

FLORENCE: You are going to ruin everything over what – booze??

CHARLES: Get off my back!

FLORENCE: Don't you have a show tonight?

CHARLES: I'll be straight by then.

FLORENCE: Will you?

CHARLES: I can handle it!

> (He drains his glass, grabs his jacket from the back of the chair, and storms out, leaving Florence alone)
>
> FADE OUT/ END OF SCENE

ACT ONE Scene 4

February 1921, the Drama League Dinner. EUGENE, is sitting on stage in the "Office" area, reading from a newspaper. He is partially dressed for a fancy night out (pants, vest), and will finish dressing (tie and jacket) during the scene.

EUGENE: (Reading)
"Charles Gilpin became the subject of controversy when, in the final ballot, he was named among the ten persons to be honored at the Drama League's annual dinner. An early ballot indicating that Gilpin was likely to be chosen as one of the ten leading stage stars who had contributed the most to the theater in the current year, raised questions by some members as to whether Gilpin should be invited at all, in view of his race... "

(CHARLES GILPIN, 40, enters from Stage Right, similar to Eugene, partially dressed for a night on the town. He carries the finishing touches of formal attire with him, drapes them over a chair, and will complete his awards dinner look as the scene progresses.)

"Some suggested that, should Gilpin's name be among those chosen, a "nice letter" should be sent to him instead of an actual invitation. This suggestion was followed by strong protests and petitions from some of the other potential nominees, who voiced their indignation against any such discrimination..."

(Eugene slams the newspaper down on his desk)

CHARLES: The honor of being chosen among the top ten is enough for me, without going to the dinner.

(Eugene and Charles meet Center Stage)

EUGENE: Oh you're going to this dinner.

23

CHARLES: Are YOU going? You're one of the ten selected.

EUGENE: I don't really believe in awards like this. It's nice to be recognized for what you do, but to say that one artist is better than another artist is ludicrous.

CHARLES: (Amused) You don't believe in awards? I don't recall you turning down that Pulitzer Prize you won for *Beyond the Horizon* last year. (Pause) You're a hypocrite.

EUGENE: No I'm not.

CHARLES:
This Drama League announcement isn't any different than the Pulitzer; you'll accept one award, but not the other?

EUGENE: The Drama League dinner is press for the sake of press, which I don't have any interest in. The Pulitzers at least are about art and recognizing the ideal as having value.

CHARLES: "Art, above all?"

EUGENE: Absolutely. Art above all. That's why you have to go to the dinner.

CHARLES: Part of me would just rather spend my time in Harlem with my friends.

EUGENE: I fought for you to be at that dinner; I petitioned members for you.

CHARLES: That wasn't for me.

EUGENE: Of course it was.

CHARLES: No... That was Eugene O'Neill, fighting for "ART." That wasn't for ME, your friend Charlie.

EUGENE: Well –

24

CHARLES: The injustice of the Drama League denying any artist admission to its organization strictly because of race is unacceptable to you.

EUGENE: Absolutely.

CHARLES: That's why you petitioned the other members to boycott the dinner! I appreciate it, Gene. You do fight for your causes. But that wasn't for me.

EUGENE: You like being intentionally combative, don't you?

CHARLES: Combative? I wouldn't say that.

EUGENE: Of course you wouldn't.

CHARLES: I'm like you -- always one to speak my mind.

EUGENE: You're certainly less civil than you used to be.

CHARLES: Yes, I'm sure you'd prefer your Negroes to be as civil as possible.

EUGENE: You're less professional, too.

CHARLES: (THIS is offensive) LESS PROFESSIONAL?

EUGENE: I'd certainly prefer my ACTORS to speak the dialogue as written in the script, and not change it according to their own personal whim.

CHARLES: I told you how I felt about that word.

EUGENE: Yes you have, many times. A Negro who can't say the word 'nigger.'

CHARLES: Not CAN'T – WON'T. It's racist!

EUGENE: It's said intentionally for the sake of the story.

25

CHARLES: But Brutus doesn't NEED to say it.

EUGENE: He DOES need to say it. He's a character. You're an actor. Speak your lines.

CHARLES: The story doesn't need it! The universal appeal that the story has is diminished every time he says that word.

EUGENE: It makes the point!

CHARLES: It makes the play about RACE and not about anything else.

EUGENE: Changing nigger to 'colored man' or 'black boy' doesn't change the context enough to matter, Charlie!

CHARLES: It matters to me! Those other words can be changed to apply to anyone; nigger only applies to colored people. The pain of that word –

EUGENE: Is exactly what I want it to be, IN MY PLAY!

CHARLES: Oh yes, your play... your beloved 'art.' It's demeaning and demoralizing!

EUGENE: If it's that badly written then why did you take the part?

CHARLES: Because I'm an actor, I can take any 'part' and transform it. I know Brutus – I AM BRUTUS – I live him, and live with him every single day. I can make any part something better; something a writer never imagined.

EUGENE: I CREATED Brutus; do you think there's any aspect of him that I haven't imagined? Every thought in his head, every blink of his eye; every sub-conscious instinct, every conscious decision... Every part of his soul is there because I put it there! You're an ACTOR, how dare you tell me what's demeaning to my creation!

CHARLES: You've said 'actor' like that several times, like 'actors' are different creatures from you. You put the words on paper, and they

26

stay words on paper until an ACTOR takes them and breathes life into them, and makes that flat character on paper REAL. Your father was a great actor; you should know that!

EUGENE: I can assure you that what you think you know about my father bears no relation to the truth.

CHARLES: People say that he was a great actor because he got to the heart of his role – he made a mediocre play something great, something people wanted to see for years.

EUGENE: So the *Emperor Jones* is – a mediocre play?

CHARLES: Your father found more in it than just what was in the script. (Pause) Brutus is shrewd – you didn't know that, did you? It's not just dumb luck that he came upon an island of ignorant Negroes, or that he double-talked them into making him their ruler. He calculated exactly where to go and how to do it, and planned the conquest of that island completely. You didn't know he was so smart, did you? I've BEEN a Pullman Porter; have you? I know how that feels. I know how it smells – you didn't know it smells, did you? It stinks. I know that smell. I brought that to Brutus!

EUGENE: I'm sorry that my mediocre play hasn't fulfilled your dream of finding the perfect role to make you a star. Oh that's right – it has.

(Eugene lets that sink in. They both regroup)

CHARLES: A star. Is that what I am now?

EUGENE: Yes.

CHARLES: What does that make you?

EUGENE: (Without hesitation) Afraid.

CHARLES: (Guard down, they are friends again)
It's not a mediocre play, Gene, I didn't mean that.

EUGENE: I know what you meant.

CHARLES: So why are you afraid?

EUGENE: It's easy to be the poor, but brilliant artist – the one that wins awards, and prizes, that the critics respect.

CHARLES: THAT'S EASY??

EUGENE: It's easy because there are no rules for that kind of an "ARTIST." You can just – create. You can do what you want, without fear. But success – this – well this is the first play that's made any real money.

CHARLES: For you or for the Players?

EUGENE: Both.

CHARLES: You have more at stake.

EUGENE: As do you... A hit changes everything.(Beat) The tour is coming at the right time.

CHARLES: I'm looking forward to touring. (Smiles) I never thought I would say that.

EUGENE: That's nearly two years on tour; you're not concerned about playing Brutus in the south?

CHARLES: Of course I am. But I'm doing it anyway.

EUGENE: Good.   (Pause) Don't change the dialogue, Charlie.

CHARLES: Gene –

EUGENE: Don't. Change. My. Dialogue. (Beat) The press will eat you up on tour.

CHARLES: I know how to handle the press.

EUGENE: You've come a long way in four months.

CHARLES: I want to represent my race well. I want more Negro parts – good parts – someday, maybe from Negro writers.

EUGENE: Not 'mediocre' parts like mine?

CHARLES: (Pause, then complete truth) I will <u>never</u> have another part like this one.

EUGENE: You will.

(Pause)

CHARLES: What am I going to do when this is over?

EUGENE: You will work. But yes, you must have Negro writers telling <u>your</u> stories. You have an incredible culture to mine from; don't just adapt 'white' plays and stories because they're supposedly 'better.' Theater won't advance with the same stories being done over and over again.

(Pause)

EUGENE: Though I must say, I think you would make a great Othello.

CHARLES: You think so?

EUGENE: Absolutely. Your presence – and your voice... it's a marvel. You would be brilliant.

CHARLES: There's no challenge in Othello; there's just the novelty of a colored man playing a colored man.

EUGENE: (Incredulous) It's Shakespeare, for God's sake.

CHARLES: (Laughs) Yes, I suppose it is.

CHARLES: (From Act 3, Scene 3 of Othello)
    "I think that thou art just and think thou art not.

29

I'll have some proof. Her name, that was as fresh
As Dian's visage, is now begrimed and black as mine own face.
If there be cords or knives, poison, or fire, or suffocating streams,
I'll not endure it."

EUGENE: You know it.

CHARLES: I do. (Pauses) Oh. You're *surprised*. (Eugene fumbles) Training for a Negro actor is Shakespeare, and 'white' plays.

EUGENE: Training?

CHARLES: We do study, actually. Just like you.

EUGENE: But, white plays...

CHARLES: We used whiteface.

EUGENE: I didn't know there WAS such a thing.

CHARLES: There is. It wouldn't cross your mind. But – We don't have Negro plays to train from. Yet.

EUGENE: Not yet. (Eugene thinks, for a minute) "Yet be content."

(Charles thinks for a minute, then continues)

CHARLES: "Oh, blood, blood, blood!"

EUGENE: "Patience, I say. Your mind may change."

CHARLES:
"Never, Iago. Like to the Pontic sea,
Whose icy current and compulsive course
Ne'er keeps retiring ebb but keeps due on
To the Propontic and the Hellespont,
Even so my bloody thoughts with violent pace
Shall ne'er look back, ne'er ebb to humble love
Till that a capable and wide revenge

Swallow them up."

EUGENE: I knew you'd be brilliant.

CHARLES: I would be brilliant in a lot of roles, Gene. (Pause) You know all that talk about 'art above all?'

EUGENE: Yes...

CHARLES: The truth is – I believe it, too.

EUGENE: I know you do.

(Beat)

CHARLES: (As he finishes dressing) I even believe what YOU do is art.

EUGENE: Now there's the Charlie I know. (Beat) I believe what you do is art. And as hard as you make it for me to say it... You're an artist.

(Eugene exits, as the lights fade out on center stage, canned applause overhead. An announcer's voice is heard announcing Charles at the Drama League dinner)

ANNOUNCER (VOICE-OVER): And to conclude this evening this incredible evening of theater, on behalf of the Drama League, I have the great pleasure of introducing the final artist to receive an award for this theater season.

(Charles walks to Center stage and takes a deep bow)

IMMEDIATE BLACKOUT

END OF ACT ONE

31

ACT TWO Scene 1

Fall, 1923 – 2 years later. The road tour of The Emperor Jones is over, and a revival is being prepared. The Emperor Jones set is in disarray, there are a few ladders and boxes of props about, and a small couch is on the set, slightly off center, along with a few folding chairs. Louis Armstrong and King Oliver are playing loudly in the background, along with the sound of some hammering.

Eugene is sitting in a chair and table set up on the side of the Emperor Jones stage. A few books, papers, and a half empty bottle, and a glass are scattered around him. After a minute of music and hammering, he stands up shakily, and angrily shouts off Stage Right.

EUGENE: Can we cut the noise please??

        (Within seconds there is silence. A long silence.
        Eugene goes back to writing)

VOICE (From Off-Backstage): Hey Gene, there's a Mr. Gilpin here to see you?

        (Eugene stops writing. He stands, puts the portfolio
        on the chair, adjusts his tie, and takes a deep breath)

EUGENE: (Calling) YES, send him in.

        (Charles enters a minute later, in his usual suit. He is
        carrying a coat and hat.)

CHARLES: You have a new stagehand.

EUGENE: You've been on the road for two years; he's not new anymore.

CHARLES: He doesn't know who I am yet.

EUGENE: (Containing some anger) No.

CHARLES: Two years on the road… It feels like it was just yesterday that we opened the show.

EUGENE: Yes it does.

CHARLES: I remember my wife being afraid that the show wouldn't last more than the original 3 weeks. And look where we are.

EUGENE: A lot has happened since the opening.

CHARLES: I wasn't here to congratulate you on winning your second Pulitzer Prize.

EUGENE: Yes, for *Anna Christie.* That one surprised me.

CHARLES: Oh, I doubt that.

EUGENE: Well… the timing of it did, anyway. (Pause) YOU met President Harding at the White House.

CHARLES: I did. He was a very nice man

(Charles smiles. There is a semi-awkward silence)

CHARLES: I won a Spingarn Medal too.

EUGENE: Yes, from… the —

CHARLES: National Association for the Advancement of Colored People.

EUGENE: Aren't we both accomplished men?

(Another awkward silence)

EUGENE: I'm sorry the tour had to be re-routed.

CHARLES: The Klan wasn't about to let a play about a Negro ordering a white man around play across the south.

EUGNE: Though I was surprised at how – strongly – they worded their point. Although, they didn't care for my response either.

CHARLES: What did you tell them?

EUGENE: I believe my exact words were, "Go Fuck Yourself."

CHARLES: Well that's certainly what I wanted to say.

EUGENE: I was sure you wouldn't mind.

CHARLES: But you still re-routed the tour.

EUGENE:
The Board and the rest of the Players thought it would be safer.

CHARLES: I would have played every city on that tour.

EUGENE: I know.

CHARLES: At least I got to play Brutus in Richmond.

EUGENE: That's your hometown?

CHARLES: Yes. My family still lives there.

EUGENE: Your family?

CHARLES: I'm one of 14 children.

EUGENE: FOURTEEN? That's….. big.

CHARLES: And noisy. And difficult.

EUGENE: It must be. I only have one brother.

CHARLES: Sounds like a dream…

EUGENE: It was… difficult.

(Silence. Charles sees Eugene's portfolio)

CHARLES: You're writing a new play?

EUGENE: Two, actually... I can't seem to get them out fast enough.

CHARLES: Critics are calling you America's most important playwright.

EUGENE: Critics say a lot of things. I'm starting to make inroads in Europe, though, so that's good.

CHARLES: You are?

EUGENE: *Anna Christie* played in London this past spring.

CHARLES: How did it do?

EUGENE: The reviews were good, but it didn't have a long run. *The Emperor Jones* should do well when it opens in London next month. (Pause) Although it didn't do well in Berlin.

CHARLES: I'm looking forward to London. The German actors couldn't pull it off?

EUGENE: Too expressionistic, I think, even for the Germans.

CHARLES: I'm not sure what that means.

EUGENE: They're Germans, so who the hell knows.

(Another awkward silence)

CHARLES: Your new plays – what are they about? Or can't you say yet...

EUGENE: One is called *Marco Millions;* it's about a Marco Polo-type figure in the Orient.

CHARLES: It has to be about more than that.

35

EUGENE: Yes… it's about capitalism, race, social classes. All the fun subjects I love.

CHARLES: Any parts for a Negro actor in that?

EUGENE: No.

CHARLES: Well what about your other play?

EUGENE: (Pause) There's a part for a Negro actor in the second play, yes.

CHARLES: What's it about?

EUGENE: It's about a Negro married to a white woman.

CHARLES: It is? Can I read it?

EUGENE: It's not done yet, Charles.

(Pause)

CHARLES: "Charles?"

EUGENE: I have someone in mind for the part.

CHARLES: Someone else?

EUGENE: His name is Paul Robeson. He just graduated from Columbia Law School.

CHARLES: A LAWYER?? Can he act?

EUGENE: He can act.

CHARLES: Oh. He can act; AND he's smart.

EUGENE: (Now it comes out) Smart enough not to change the dialogue in my plays…

CHARLES: Gene –

EUGENE: Did you think I wouldn't find out that you had your way with my script?

CHARLES: I didn't 'have my way' with it –

EUGENE: You couldn't wait to get the play on the road, could you? Do you know some of the stagehands call you Emperor Charles? You thought you were free to change the play the way YOU wanted.

CHARLES: You know I won't say that word!

EUGENE: Yes, THAT word, you've said that many times. But you didn't change just that word, did you, Charles?

CHARLES: (Lying) I don't know what you're talking about.

EUGENE: Oh, you don't know what I'm talking about?

CHARLES: (Lying) NO...

EUGENE: Whole sections of dialogue were different!

CHARLES: I had to fix that script!

EUGENE: You had to – "FIX" – the script???

CHARLES: I had to fix your MEDIOCRE script – you really see Negroes as shiftless criminals, and savages...it's a racist, stereotype!

EUGENE: THAT is exactly what it is supposed to be!

CHARLES: So you KNOW it, and you won't change it?

EUGENE: Not one word. And I won't allow you to change any of my words, either.

CHARLES: Your words, your words – I'm so sick of hearing about your WORDS! You just wrote the damned play, I brought it to life! *I* created Brutus!

EUGENE: Oh that's right, there wouldn't BE a Brutus Jones without you.

CHARLES: It wouldn't be what it is now without me, no!

EUGENE: You've just taken over every aspect of this show, haven't you?

CHARLES: No performance was EVER impacted! Every review on the entire tour was great!

(Eugene gets in Charles's face)

EUGENE: That's not even the point anymore, Charles – you're out of control!

CHARLES: Gene...

EUGENE: You're drunk.

CHARLES: I'm not drunk.

EUGENE: I can smell it!

(In these next exchanges, while both men are agitated, Charles who indeed has been drinking, becomes more manic)

CHARLES: You can barely stand.

EUGENE: My drinking is under control.

CHARLES: Yes, I can see that.

EUGENE: There's no professionalism left in you anymore, is there?

CHARLES: (To himself) Florence was right...

EUGENE: What are you talking about?

CHARLES: My wife. She said a long time ago that there would be a cost to playing Brutus. I told her the cost didn't matter.

EUGENE: What cost? Brutus is the role of a lifetime, you should be grateful to have it.

CHARLES: Grateful.

EUGENE: Yes!!

CHARLES: At the "cost" of my dignity?! No. NO! I spent most of my career fighting the stereotype of the Negro. I REFUSED to perform in musicals, to be on stage in Negro revues, dancing and grinning like a fool. I REFUSED to sing those ridiculous songs. I REFUSED to perform in blackface – to do ANYTHING to demean my race! And now, this play – does it for me. I may as well wear actual black face now!

> (Charles goes to an open makeup box on the stage and grabs black shoe polish)

CHARLES:
Or is that what you wanted all along? (He smears shoe polish on his face.) Is that black enough for you?

EUGENE: That's not what I want, and you know it! Plenty of white actors wanted this part – *I CHOSE YOU*. Because once upon a time you DID bring something amazing to this part. And because ART matters!

CHARLES: ART!

EUGENE: Yes, ART, above fucking ALL. And you... (Pause) You – were brilliant. Once. Now you're all ham and cheap theatrics.

CHARLES: Like your father?

(This hits O'Neill)

EUGENE: You're not good for anything anymore. And the only thing you take seriously is yourself.

(Both men stare each other down)

EUGENE: I went out on a limb for you. I gave you chances I would've NEVER given anyone else, and I've put up with you more than I ever have anyone else. (Pause) I <u>liked</u> you, Charlie. That ends today.

CHARLES: What do you mean?

EUGENE: Oh you're fired.

CHARLES: EXCUSE ME??

EUGENE: You're. FIRED.

CHARLES: You can't fire me!

EUGENE: Oh I can. It's MY play.

CHARLES: You don't HAVE a play without me!

EUGENE: Do you honestly think I'm going to take you to London to represent me and my play?

CHARLES: This play would be nothing without me, and you know it!

EUGENE: NO London run, NO revival – you're out.

CHARLES: We have a contract!

EUGENE: The contract hasn't been signed, my lawyer can get me out of that.

CHARLES: Who are you going to get? Somebody in blackface??

EUGENE: I'll call Paul Robeson.

CHARLES: A lawyer, for God's sake?

EUGENE: He'll do it in a second.

CHARLES: A no-name actor!

EUGENE: He was first on the list to play Brutus 3 years ago.

(The tom-tom begins. Faster, stronger)

EUGENE: You didn't know that, did you? You weren't the first choice for that part.

(Charles hears the drum, hears Eugene, and tries to collect himself)

EUGENE: He didn't want it then, but he desperately wants it now.

CHARLES: Oh I'm SURE he does! Now that I've made something of it... I made it the best part for a Negro actor EVER, and now he wants it? He can't have it!

EUGENE: We are done.

(Eugene turns, picks up his portfolio, and storms towards the exit at Stage Right)

CHARLES: He can't have it!

EUGENE: (Calling behind him as he exits) You're done.

CHARLES: GENE!

(Charles starts to follow Eugene – he closes his eyes, breathing furiously, then runs off stage)

BLACKOUT/ END OF ACT ONE

ACT TWO Scene 2

March, 1924, 6 months later. At Center Stage, the Emperor Jones set is back to performance-level shape, no scattered ladders, props, or chairs save one folder chair angled facing Stage Right. The stage is empty.

After a minute, Eugene, carrying his portfolio, enters from up Stage Left and comes down to center. As he comes down he adjusts some random piece of the set, looks at it, and then sits in the chair and begins writing.

After another minute, Florence Gilpin enters. She is wearing her good coat and hat, and carries a purse.

FLORENCE: Excuse me.

(Eugene is lost in writing and doesn't hear her)

FLORENCE: Mr. O'Neill?

(He stops, rubs his eyes, and looks up)

EUGENE: Can I help you?

FLORENCE:
You don't remember me...

EUGENE: I'm sorry...

FLORENCE: I'm Florence Gilpin. Charles's wife?

EUGENE: Oh I'm sorry... yes, Mrs. Gilpin. It's been a few years since we met, forgive me for not recognizing you.

FLORENCE: We only met once; on the opening night of *The Emperor Jones*. I came to a few performances but didn't see you again.

EUGENE: No, I go to the rehearsals but I don't attend any shows after opening night.

FLORENCE: Why?

EUGENE: Rehearsals I can impact – performances I cannot. Performances are not for playwrights, or men with weak stomachs. I, unfortunately, am both.

FLORENCE: (Smiling) Yes, of course.

EUGENE: (Getting her a chair) Ah, now I recognize you; that beautiful smile.

FLORENCE: (Flattered, but aware, she sits down) Words are your living, aren't they?

EUGENE: Indeed they are. (Pause) What can I do for you?

FLORENCE: (Mustering her courage) I'd like to convince you to talk to Charles.

(Pause)

EUGENE: I'm – I'm sorry but there isn't anything I can do for Charles.

FLORENCE: You're opening a revival of *The Emperor Jones* in less than a month.

EUGENE: It's not a full revival, it's just a few anniversary performances, to set the stage for my new play.

FLORENCE: *All God's Chillun' Got Wings.*

EUGENE: You keep up with theater news.

FLORENCE: Theater is everything to Charles. He'd die if he couldn't act.

EUGENE: He is a very talented man. I'm sure he will find – work...

FLORENCE: Not work like yours.

EUGENE: I heard he was in a production of *Roseanne* that's running now.

FLORENCE: The original cast of *Roseanne* was an all-white cast, in blackface. Someone decided it would be... 'interesting' to do a play about Negroes with Negro actors, so now there's a revival.

EUGENE: It's work.

FLORENCE: It's not good work. Not like yours.

EUGENE: (Pause) I'm not sure what you think I can do.

FLORENCE: You're the greatest playwright in America.

EUGENE: And Charles is stubborn, arrogant, and hot-tempered.

FLORENCE: It seems to me I've heard the same things said about you, Mr. O'Neill.

EUGENE: (This stings) You flatter me, madam.

FLORENCE: (Resigned) It wasn't meant to flatter either one of you.

EUGENE: I see.

FLORENCE: I know where it comes from. His parents were born slaves, but after the war and Emancipation, they made something of themselves, they worked hard. His father worked in a steel mill, and his mother became a nurse, she worked at the City Hospital in Richmond. He got a good education for a colored boy, and went to Catholic school. He quit school to help his family, and got a job apprenticing at a newspaper. He got the theater bug... and joined a few minstrel shows.

EUGENE: And where do you come from?

FLORENCE: Me? Oh I'm just a city girl. Nothing special.

EUGENE: I don't believe that – at all.

FLORENCE: Well... my grandparents were born slaves, but they escaped and made it north through the Underground Railroad. They settled in Philiadelphia, that's where they raised their family. That's where I was born.

EUGENE: How did you meet Charles?

FLORENCE: He was a janitor for a while, and I was a maid in the same building. I fell in love with him the minute I saw him. HE took a little convincing.

EUGENE: I doubt that.

FLORENCE: He did. He said he wasn't sure he was the marrying kind.

EUGENE: He's a passionate actor; it would surprise me if he weren't equally as passionate about women.

FLORENCE: He cares – too much, if that's possible. He's a fighter, you know – one of fourteen kids, he had to fight all his life – for clothes, for food, for attention... for respect. He had to know what he wanted and how to get it, very early. That's a hard habit to break. He's been disappointed a lot in his life.

EUGENE: I know a little about that. (Silence) Does he know you're here?

FLORENCE: NO, he doesn't. (Eugene nods) Your new play –

EUGENE: It stars Paul Robeson.

FLORENCE: *The Emperor Jones* special performances?

EUGENE: He is handling those as well.

FLORENCE: This Paul Robeson – is he that good?

45

(Long Pause)

EUGENE: He's – not Charles.

FLORENCE: I see... (Pause) What about your new play? The one you're writing now?

EUGENE: *Desire Under the Elms* is about a white family in New England; it's based on a Greek tragedy.

FLORENCE: (More to herself) Nothing for Charles...

EUGENE: No.

FLORENCE: If you could – if I could convince him to talk to you in per –

EUGENE: It won't help.

FLORENCE: PLEASE.

>(They have connected, and they look in each other deeply)

EUGENE: You love him a great deal.

(Pause. (Florence implores him with her eyes for a long time; then knows the battle is over)

FLORENCE: I won't keep you.

>(Eugene nods. Florence turns her back to him to exit)

EUGENE: Goodbye, Mrs. Gilpin.

>(Florence stops. She doesn't turn back to look at Eugene. She breathes, and continues her exit. Eugene watches her exit and looks in that direction long after she has gone. Then he paces.)

(Lights lower slowly on Center Stage and Eugene, and come up brightly on the Stage Right kitchen area, so both areas are lit for a time. As the lights rise on the kitchen, Charles enters, pacing, so both men are pacing at the same time. Charles sits down. He stands, paces, and finally sits down again. As Charles sits the last time, the lights lower and be out on Center Stage and Eugene exits in the dark)

Florence enters, in her coat and hat; she has just come from meeting with Eugene)

CHARLES: Where have you been?

FLORENCE: Walking; I needed a walk.

CHARLES: You've been on your feet all day, but you needed a walk?

FLORENCE: I did. Is there something wrong with that? (Silence) Are you hungry? I can put something on...

CHARLES: I can't eat.

FLORENCE: Did you eat today?

CHARLES: I'm not hungry, can you please stop already?

FLORENCE: (Takes off her coat and hat) All right. (Silence) Why are you home? Shouldn't you be at the theater?

CHARLES: I hate that show.

FLORENCE: It's work.

CHARLES: It's degrading.

FLORENCE: You can't be picky right now.

CHARLES: The stage manager hates me. They all hate me.

FLORENCE: What happened?

CHARLES: The director doesn't know what he's doing.

FLORENCE: Charles...

CHARLES: They let me go.

FLORENCE: Oh my God...

CHARLES: I just wanted that show to be the best it could be.

FLORENCE: We talked about that; you can't tell a director what to do!

CHARLES: I made it better than it was!

FLORENCE: Can you talk to him? Can you get the part back?

CHARLES: They've already replaced me.

FLORENCE: That fast

CHARLES: That fast!

FLORENCE: Who did they get that fast?

(Charles doesn't answer)

FLORENCE: CHARLES!

CHARLES: ROBESON.

FLORENCE: Paul Robeson...

CHARLES: He is <u>EVERYWHERE</u>! I can't get away from him!

FLORENCE: It's not his fault –

48

CHARLES: He's taking my leftovers!

FLORENCE: He must be a good actor.

CHARLES: Whose side are you on, Florence?

FLORENCE: I'm on your side, baby, but we don't have to tear down another colored man trying to make his own way, like you did.

CHARLES: I made *The Emperor Jones* the part of a lifetime and now he wants it.

FLORENCE: I want you to go to that theater and ask for your job back.

CHARLES: No.

FLORENCE: Honey, you have to work!

CHARLES: I REFUSE to sacrifice who I am for a part in a play! How can I just walk in that door?

FLORENCE: What choice do you have? If you have something else lined up, please tell me!

CHARLES: Maybe we'll move to Philadelphia. There's good theater for Negroes coming up there, and there's a film company forming that I could be part of....

FLORENCE: Movies?

CHARLES: What's wrong with movies?

FLORENCE: Aren't you tired of chasing jobs around the country?

CHARLES: That's an actor's life, honey, you go where the jobs are. You knew that when you married me.

FLORENCE: I thought you wanted to settle down someplace, for the baby's sake.

CHARLES: I want…. (trails off) How do I make you understand? (Beat) Ever since I was a boy, I wanted to do something – that mattered. Something important, that would last, beyond me – maybe beyond my time on this earth. And I KNEW I would make that happen. I didn't know how it would happen, or what it would be – but I knew it would happen. That play… changed me. Brutus – is a buffoon. Do you think I don't know that? He's everything reprehensible to us, to our race. I know what it means to shut my eyes, and put on a mask, and play THAT character. But I've made him better. I've made this play BETTER. It may be the greatest thing I'll ever do. OR, it may be just the beginning of things to come. I'm a great actor, and I know it, Florence. I. KNOW. It. And now that I've had a taste of… Greatness? I can't go back to… playing slaves! If I were white, a DOZEN chances would have come my way from this. Look where we are now.

FLORENCE: Yes, Charles – LOOK where we are! I've been working 2 jobs since you were fired from *The Emperor Jones*, we're barely making it. I can't keep us going on my own. (Pause) I won't.

(He takes her hand from across the kitchen table)

CHARLES: I know I can do more. And I KNOW I'm worthy of more. And some little minstrel show like *Roseanne* isn't where I can be great.

FLORENCE: You told me you were gonna play the game; that you KNEW how to behave, and you were going to play the game.

CHARLES: I did that for a while. But – I can't now. It's beneath me. How do I settle for that?

FLORENCE: I don't know – but I know you need to find a way. Because if you can't do the minor things like *Roseanne*? No one is going to give you a chance to do the great things like *The Emperor Jones* ever again.

(Charles is silent, lets go of her hand)

FLORENCE: So are you going to go talk to the producers?

(After a long silence, Charles leans back in his chair)

(Florence exits)

BLACKOUT
END OF SCENE

ACT TWO Scene 3

It's November, 1926, 2 years later. Lights come up on the down
Stage Left area of the stage, which had been the Drama League
dinner area. The podium and main Drama League elements have
been removed and replaced with a very small table, folding chair,
and lamp – an office area in the theater which Eugene is using. He is
seated at the table facing Stage Left, his back to Center Stage.

After a time Charles enters, slowly. Still well dressed, his demeanor is
reserved, his usual confidence gone. He has reached bottom.

He stands center, watching Eugene write for a time, hoping he will
turn around but Eugene is intent on writing.

CHARLES: (Softly) Eugene. (Eugene keeps writing) (Charles steps
closer) Hello?

> (Eugene finally stops, frustrated)

EUGENE:
WHAT!?

> (He turns around)

EUGENE:
Oh. Charles.

CHARLES:
Hello.

> (Extended silence)

EUGENE:
It's been a long time.

CHARLES:
It has.

> (Both are waiting for the other to say something;
> then the speak simultaneously)

EUGENE:

(Together with Charles)

What are you doing –

CHARLES:

(Together with Eugene)

How have you –

EUGENE:
I'm sorry, you –

CHARLES:
No, no...

(Eugene motions for him to continue)

CHARLES:

(Finally)

How have you been?

EUGENE:
Good.

(Pause)

CHARLES:
I heard you had another baby. You and your wife.

EUGENE:

(Not expecting that)

Uh, we did... a girl. (Pause) And then we split up.

CHARLES:
Oh. I'm sorry.

EUGENE:
What are you doing here?

CHARLES:

I – came to talk to you.

EUGENE:
Alright...

(Charles changes the subject)

CHARLES:
What are you working on?

EUGENE:
There's not a part for you in it, Charles.

(Pause. Now Eugene changes the subject)

EUGENE:
What are you doing these days?

CHARLES:
I need a favor – from an old friend.

EUGENE:
An old – "friend..."

CHARLES:
(Pauses – thinks)
A fellow artist?

(No response)

CHARLES:
Please, Gene.

(Eugene pauses, then nods. He exits, quickly
returning with another folding chair that he unfolds.
Charles doesn't sit down just yet)

EUGENE:
What do you have to say?

CHARLES:
I – I need work.

EUGENE:
You do...

CHARLES:
I do.

EUGENE:
You should have thought about that three years ago.

CHARLES:
I should have.

EUGENE:
What happened to you?

CHARLES:
YOU happened to me.

EUGENE:
I happened to you.

CHARLES:
Why did you write that play?

EUGENE:
So you're giving me credit for writing the play now.

CHARLES:
I – I always gave you credit for writing it.

EUGENE:
Oh you did.

CHARLES:
I know what it did for me. For US.

(Eugene paces for a minute)

EUGENE:
If you had just followed my script, Charlie...

CHARLES:
I know...

EUGENE:
If you'd have just said the words.

CHARLES:
Yes.

EUGENE:
ALL of the words.

> (Charles takes it)

EUGENE:
You know, a part of me – admired – your conviction. You didn't betray what you believed was right, no matter the consequences. And they have been severe.

CHARLES:
THANK YOU.

> (Pause)

EUGENE:
I might never have used Paul Robeson.

CHARLES:
He's a fine young man.

EUGENE:
He's a good actor, and a better man. I have tremendous respect for Paul as a person. (Pause) But there was something about YOU...

> (Eugene looks at Charles intently)

EUGENE:
He wasn't you.

CHARLES:
How did your father do it?

EUGENE:
Do what?

CHARLES:
You said *The Count of Monte Christo* destroyed your father. How did he live with himself?

EUGENE:
There is debate whether he did live with himself. In public he was the consummate citizen and pillar of the community. In private... His soul died years before he did.

CHARLES:
But he left a great legacy behind him.

EUGENE:
We all worry about our legacy.

CHARLES:
Your legacy is that you're the greatest playwright in America. What's my legacy? (Pause) I want – I wanted to leave something like that behind me.

EUGENE:
I heard you've been involved in setting up several Negro theater groups. You're leaving something behind.

CHARLES:
Not that kind of legacy. Something more – permanent – than that.

(Pause)

EUGENE:
What exactly do you want?

CHARLES:
(Mustering his courage)
I want to do a revival of *The Emperor Jones*.

EUGENE:
YOU want to do a revival?

CHARLES:
Yes. I'd like to direct it.

EUGENE:
And not play Brutus?

CHARLES:
I'd play Brutus too. I'd do both.

EUGENE:
OH… I don't know about that. You doing both?

CHARLES:
Do you think I can't do both?

EUGENE:
What I think doesn't matter.

CHARLES:
No, I'd like to know what you think.

EUGENE:
(Pause)
Honestly… I think… that you would do a great job.

CHARLES:
So you'll let me do it?

EUGENE:
No.

CHARLES:

WHY?

EUGENE:
Because I can't trust you, Charlie. Tell me how I trust you EVER again.

CHARLES:
There's too much to lose if I don't do this right. I want to remind people how good I was, so that I can work again.

EUGENE:
You can't recapture past glory.

CHARLES:
I don't want to recapture anything. (Pause) I want – I NEED – to play Brutus again.

>(This affects Eugene. He stands and walks slowly to center stage)

EUGENE:
You sound like my father.

CHARLES:
How?

EUGENE:
I think that the part of The Count wasn't just work to him... it was like a friend that he had to crawl into, and feel – from the inside.

CHARLES:
Yes, exactly... from the inside.

EUGENE:
Yes...

>(Pause from Eugene, as he thinks)

EUGENE:
The last revival wasn't that long ago.

CHARLES:
Long enough.

(Eugene thinks, walks through the stage area)

CHARLES:
Please, Gene.

(Pause)

EUGENE:
Don't make me regret it, Charlie. If you blow this – you're finished forever.

CHARLES
I understand.

(Pause)

EUGENE:
I'm going to have to insist that you stick to the script.

CHARLES:
I will.

EUGENE:
You won't change a word.

CHARLES:
I WON'T.

EUGENE:
Not one word. Not even nigger. You'll say it every time.

(Charles nods)

EUGENE:
I'm going to have to have your word.

(Charles begins to speak, then stops himself)

CHARLES:
Okay.

EUGENE:
That's not good enough.

(Charles faces Eugene. They look at each other)

CHARLES:
I promise I won't change a word.

(Eugene looks at Charles intently)

EUGENE:
I'm going to need to hear you say it.

(Silence, as Charles understands what Eugene wants)

EUGENE:
SAY IT.

(LONG PAUSE, as Charles considers... everything; history... his own conviction... Florence. He decides to say it)

CHARLES:
(Plainly)
Nigger.

EUGENE:
(Takes a deep breath)
You have your revival.

A crash of drums and tom-toms, incredibly loud. Through the drumbeats, Charles is changed on stage by Florence and Eugene into his Brutus Jones costume. They swirl around him in a flurry, taking off his vest and jacket, putting on his Emperor's coat, gun, and other props.

Florence and Eugene leave Charles alone on the empty stage, the music ends abruptly as it started. He stands alone on the empty stage. The tom-tom that Brutus hears in the scene is audible to the audience.

He has no energy, no focus. He is ALL the 'ham and cheap theatrics' that Eugene called him earlier. Everything he did brilliantly in Act 1, Scene 3, to great effect is the exact opposite now, and he drops in and out of the role.

Text in italics and boldface is Charles's own voice as he's dropping in and out of character, talking to himself.

BRUTUS:

"What time's it getting' to be.
I dassent light no match to find out.
No wait – I wonder, I forgot I wonder….
WHAT TIME'S IT GETTING' TO BE, I WONDER?
I dassent light no match to find out. Phoo! It's warm an' dat's a fac! [Wearily] How long I been makin' tracks in dese woods? Must be hours an' hours.
Seems like, ***seems like, seems like, yes…*** Seems LIKE fo'evah!

Yit can't be, when dey moon's jes' riz. [Charles mechanically points to a "moon"]

Majesty! ***There's no majesty in this baby now.*** [Charles sobs, then pulls himself together quickly]

Never min… It's all part o'le game. Dis night come to an end like everything else. And when you gits dar safe and has dat bankroll in yo' hands you laughs at all dis.

[He starts to whistle but checks himself abruptly]. What yo whistlin' for, you po' dope? Want all de worl' to heah you? [He stops talking to listen]

The drum, yes – hear the drum, I hear it...

That drum, it Sho gits nearer from de sound. Dey're packin it along wid 'em. Time fo' me to move. [He takes a step forward, then stops, worriedly] What's dat odd clickety sound I heah?

Dere it is! Sound close! Sound like – sound like – Fo'God sake, so und like some –

[Charles pauses]

Ni... *[Charles stops completely. Here it is.]*–

It sounds like some – Ni... *[AND NOW, IN HIS OWN VOICE, SHOUTING]*

IT SOUNDS LIKE SOME COLORED BOY!

[As soon as Charles says "COLORED BOY" he knows it's over]

(The tom-tom stops on 'Colored Boy,' the last beat deliberately loud)

(The drum is gone. Brutus is gone)

CHARLES: (This is Charles)Where's the drum? Where's that tom-tom?

>   *(Florence enters upstage Right, behind Charles, out*
>   *of his sight. Eugene enters opposite her, upstage*
>   *Left, out of Charles sight. They watch his collapse)*
>
>   *(Charles tries to pick back up with the monologue...*
>   *but his heart is gone)*

CHARLES:
(Spins around, trying to find the drum, asking the audience)
WAIT!!

Where's the drum? Where's the tom-tom, the drum... Where's that tom-tom, Where's the drum, Where's that tom-tom, Where's the drum, Where's the tom-tom......

> [Charles stands center, then drops to his knees, in the quiet. And sobs.]

CHARLES:
I'm sorry.... I'm sorry.....

> (Florence goes to Charles, and helps him up. They begin to exit the stage.
>
> As Florence leads Charles off stage, he spots Eugene. He stops crying, wipes his face, faces Eugene and defiantly straightens himself, fixes his jacket. He is proud. Florence and Charles exit. Eugene exits opposite.
>
> BLACKOUT
>
> END OF SCENE

ACT TWO
EPILOGUE

1930. Charles's grave. Lights come up slowly, the stage is empty.
Eugene is standing center stage, in a dark suit, looking down towards
down Center Stage. After a minute, Florence enters, in black,
carrying flowers. She stops when she sees Eugene, looks around,
turns around – then changes her mind, and turns back. She walks
slowly down Center Stage, and stands near to Eugene, also looking
down.

FLORENCE:
Mr. O'Neill.

EUGENE:
Mrs. Gilpin – I thought everyone had gone.

FLORENCE:
I'm a little surprised to see you here.

EUGENE:
I didn't want to intrude.

FLORENCE:
You are intruding.

EUGENE:
I'm just here to pay respect to Charles.

FLORENCE: You're a little late for that, don't you think?

EUGENE: I may be.

(Pause)

FLORENCE:
I'm sorry, that was rude of me.

EUGENE:

I deserved it.

FLORENCE:
Charles wouldn't have liked it. He was so proper; he hated rudeness.

EUGENE:
I can think of a few rude things he said to me.

FLORENCE:
Well as you said... you probably deserved them.

(They both look forward, at the grave)

(Beat)

EUGENE:
The last time we met, you asked me to give Charles another chance.

FLORENCE:
A chance you didn't give him.

EUGENE:
No. Not then.

FLORENCE:
You made him crawl to you and BEG for another chance.

EUGENE:
I thought you weren't going to be rude.

FLORENCE:
Charles is dead. Who is it going to hurt now?

(No reply from Eugene)

FLORENCE:
Do you know who He was? He was a leading member of the Anita Bush Players, one of the first Negro theater companies in America. He STARRED in over a hundred productions with the Lafayette Players in Harlem. He was already a legend in the Negro community

but in one night – opening night of your play – he became the most important Negro man in the country. In the whole country. He couldn't walk down the street without people stopping him to shake his hand, or say "Thank You." Sculptors wanted him to model for them; he was called "the Moses of the Negro" by leading Negro newspapers.

EUGENE:
I didn't know all that.

FLORENCE:
Of course not; you never bothered to know about him. (Pause) How much money did Charles make for you?

EUGENE:
I – don't know...

FLORENCE:
Charles was paid $50 a week for your play. That's a lot of money for a Negro – but I'm guessing you and the Provincetown Players made a lot more than that.

EUGENE:
We did, yes.

FLORENCE
When Charles went to the White House, President Harding wanted to talk about the struggles of Race relations in this country – with HIM. He wanted Charles to be an Ambassador for the Negro, and advance the cause for all of us. Have YOU been to the White House, Mr. O'Neill?

EUGENE:
No. I haven't.

FLORENCE:
No you haven't.

(Beat)

FLORENCE:
But this is the man that you humiliated – that you made crawl and beg for a job in a play that HE made famous – for you.

(Pause)

EUGENE:
I understand you.

FLORENCE:
Do you?

EUGENE:
I do, Mrs. Gilpin. But remember – Charles wasn't blameless in all this.

FLORENCE:
No – he wasn't. I believe you once called him "stubborn, arrogant, and hot-tempered."

EUGENE:
You called me the same, as I recall.

FLORENCE:
(Smiles slightly)
I did.

(Long Pause. We feel that they are out of things to say to each other)

EUGENE:
My father was an actor. He was the most – (Pauses, acknowledging her) he was just as famous as Charles was. He never went to the White House either, but he couldn't walk down the street without being stopped. Everyone loved him in the one role that made him a star. But they wouldn't let him do anything else. First he needed it for the money; and, he was safe in that role. Then it scared him, to think he couldn't do anything else. Then he resented it, for robbing him of his talent. By the end he hated it.

FLORENCE:
I don't think Charles *hated* Brutus.

EUGENE:
He would have. Eventually.

FLORENCE:
I'm not so sure.

EUGENE:
One of the last things my father said to me before he died was that
Monte Christo was a curse, and that he wished he'd never taken that
part.

FLORENCE:
You think *The Emperor Jones* was Charles' curse?

EUGENE:
Wasn't it?

FLORENCE:
I asked him once if he was prepared to play Brutus no matter the
cost.

EUGENE:
What did he say?

FLORENCE:
"The character may not be worthy, but the role is."

EUGENE:
He implied other things about that role to me. But – he was the
consummate actor.

FLORENCE:
You say that now that he's gone. It would have been nice for him to
have heard that from you when it mattered.

EUGENE:
One of many regrets, believe me.

FLORENCE:

The only curse for Charles was that he had no other options. Your father at least had the option to do other work; to fail as many times as he wanted, even if it wasn't successful. Charles had one chance – your play. There was nothing for him after that.

EUGENE:
There are Negro playwrights; Willis Richardson... Langston Hughes...

FLORENCE:
By the time those writers came along, his chance was gone. Charles was ahead of his time.

> (Florence takes her flowers, and steps up as far downstage Center as she can. She lays the flowers on the 'grave,' and then steps back beside Eugene).

FLORENCE:
Now what?

EUGENE:
Now we say goodbye.

(They face each other. Eugene extends his hand. She takes it)

> (As they shake hands, Charles enters well behind them, in his dress suit from Act 1-Scene 1, dressed for the Drama League dinner, looking sharp. He watches them.)

EUGENE:
Of all the actors who ever played in my plays, only one ever fully realized a part as I heard it in my head, as I wrote it and imagined it from the beginning – that was Charles Gilpin.

FLORENCE:
Now he's left to history.

EUGENE:
As we all are. Whatever the reckoning.

FLORENCE:
Your place is secure. How will history remember HIM?

EUGENE:
History won't forget him.

FLORENCE:
It already has.

> (Florence turns toward the "grave" and recites)

FLORENCE:
"Rest on, rest through all eternity;
Sleep the much-deserved sleep
And when the great day shall come
Without the wearied beat of the tom-tom
Or the rumbling of some drum,
But from the blast of Gabriel's horn,
Arise."

> (Florence and Eugene turn and exit on opposite sides
> of the stage. Charles watches them leave, and then
> comes down center stage.)

CHARLES:
What did Shakespeare say about time? "Make use of time – let not
advantage slip."

I tried to use my time – there just wasn't enough OF it. I knew I had
to be ready, whenever my chance came. And I was. Mr. O'Neill wrote
a play for a Negro, and I got a chance to do what I had dreamed of all
my life. It was glorious. But all dreams die, as they must.

Things didn't change as much as I thought they would, right away....
Shuffle Along and other Negro revues became the rage; but there
weren't much more than minstrel shows, just fancied up. I didn't fit
with that 'style.' My own people thought my work was too
'highbrow' and when white people wanted an actor, they still hired a
white man. Blackface didn't end with me. Some people still do it,
even now – as a joke. The work I did get after Brutus was insulting.

But *imagine*...

(His voice trails off)

I tried not to let it bother me – it didn't make any difference to me if people didn't like me, Charlie Gilpin, personally. Rather, I wanted them to look at my work; if it was Art, I want them to applaud it. If it was not, then let them condemn it. If my work had the merit of making me remembered for having entertained, instructed, and stimulated thought to the slightest degree, I am satisfied.

But Imagine – what could have been...

(Charles ends his monologue Center Stage)

BLACKOUT, then immediately:

ANNOUNCER (VOICE-OVER): And to conclude this evening this incredible evening of theater, on behalf of the Drama League, I have the great pleasure of introducing the final artist to receive an award for this theater season. Ladies and Gentlemen, Mr. Charles S. Gilpin!

(Spotlight on Charles, as tight as possible, as canned, thunderous applause fill the theater. He bows, smiles. Finally the applause fades)

(Finally, Charles gives his Drama League acceptance speech, from Act 1 Scene 4)

CHARLES:
Thank you all so much, and thank you to the Drama League and all the members who voted to accord me this award. It is an honor to be among you, and to feel part of this community. I want my friends to remember that I am honestly striving to present my ART rather than myself to the public, and in this endeavor I have received the greatest encouragement and courtesy. A close-up of Charles Gilpin does not look very inviting.

In the future, I shall try to make my work stand out as prominently, if that is within my power.

An "artist", I always thought, was something a long, long way off. I never expected to reach that height, but you have called me that. I am so glad if I have given you an evening of pleasure, and I am happy to be among you and have you know my work. Now that I am here, among fellow artists and, if I may I say, colleagues... know that I will always strive to produce work equally as praiseworthy – and equally as important.

(He pauses)

And now, THIS poor player has strutted, and fretted his hour upon the stage. I'll be heard no more.

(Applause fills the air, grows louder, and Charles looks around as he bows, as the lights fade out on the applause)

FADEOUT

THE END

Author's Notes

When planning the structure of this play, I originally thought that this would be a good play to do in rep with *The Emperor Jones*. The actor playing Brutus would play Charles, and the actor playing Smithers would play Eugene.

Music of that decade (Louis Armstrong's Hot Five and Hot Seven bands, King Oliver, Benny Goodman, Fletcher Henderson, Bessie Smith, Bix Biederbecke, Clara Smith) should be played where possible.

www.ingramcontent.com/pod-product-compliance
Lightning Source LLC
Chambersburg PA
CBHW071747090426
42738CB00011B/2587